BUILDING PARENT-TEACHER PARTNERSHIPS

INTENTIONAL CONNECTIONS

DOROTHY HARMAN

Building Parent Teacher Partnerships:

Intentional Connections

Written by: Dorothy Harman

Published by: Parent Child Press

Copyright 2022 Dorothy Harman

ISBN# 978-0-939195-71-8

A Division of Montessori Services

www.montessoriservices.com

Dear Readers,

Hello, I am Dorothy Harman. I have been a classroom teacher working with parents like you for decades and I am very pleased to meet you. My journey began when I was 4 years old and Sesame Street appeared on one of four channels of my parents' awkwardly boxy and oversized television. I was enthralled—there was laughter, singing, learning and lots of lessons about friendship. My childhood dream was to grow up, work on Sesame Street and be a "muppeteer". Well, I missed the goal a little, although I have had the privilege of working with families and children and sharing a great deal of laughter, singing, learning and lots of lessons on friendships. This book is for families in celebration of their relationships with their children's teachers and begins with a little wisdom from the master muppeteer.

> The attitude you have as a parent is what your kids will learn from more than what you tell them. They don't remember what you try to teach them. They remember what you are.
>
> —Jim Henson

I celebrate you and "what you are" for picking this copy of *Intentional Connections: Building Parent Teacher Partnerships* and I wish you lots of laughter, singing, learning and lessons on friendship.

In partnership,

Dorothy Harman

Dorothy Harman

This book is dedicated to my greatest and most beloved teachers, my children Alicia and Anthony, and to the many teachers who partnered with me in their development. And to my husband, Chris, who chose to parent them, too.

Contents

Prologue vii

How This Book Works (so you will not have to) ix

Chapter I: It Takes a Village 1

   Not to "Should" on You 4

   Why Parent and Teacher Engagement Matters 5

   Childhood as Observed by Dr. Maria Montessori................ 6

   Some Parenting Basics 8

Chapter II: The Relationship Between Adults: Fostering Community 11

   Trust 11

   Communication 13

   Be ~~Involved~~, Better Yet…Be Engaged 16

Chapter III: The Relationship with the Child: Fostering Growth 19

   Autonomy 19

   Accountability 22

   Intellectual Development 25

Chapter IV: The Relationship with the Environment: Removing Obstacles 29

   Discretion: Little Pitchers, Big Ears 29

   Technology 32

   Play 35

Chapter V: Partnership: A Word of Appreciation 38

References..41

Suggested Resources..43

  For Ideas on Discipline in the Classroom and Home:........ 43

  For More Inspiration: 43

Acknowledgments 44

About the Author 45

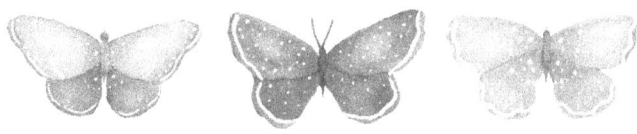

Prologue

When a tiny caterpillar emerges from an egg, it seems like a pretty simple journey to become a butterfly. It eats a little; it crawls a little bit and in time it builds its chrysalis. Then within that hard shell, a transformation occurs and out emerges a beautiful butterfly. It rests; it spreads its wings, it flies, and the process begins again with a tiny egg.

It seems simple enough.

But, it is not simple at all, the conditions have to be just right and the environment suitable for the seemingly miraculous metamorphosis to occur, yet more often than not this beautiful act of nature occurs without notice.

Is it possible that we take relationships for granted as well, as simply occurring without care to the environment or without intention?

In 2018, I had the privilege to write my first book, *Intentional Connections: A Practical Guide to Parent Engagement in Early Childhood and Lower Elementary Classrooms* and present to educator audiences who were anxious to connect with the families of the children in their classrooms. One question continued to resurface from those listeners, "Do you have a companion book to share with parents?"

It seemed evident to me that there was a need for a conversation between educators and parents. That dialogue could be centered on the wisdom, experience, training, and understanding of children that educators implement daily and the deep love a parent or caregiver has for their child. Those very children are delivered to schools and care settings by families who entrust the education professionals to guide the skills that the child will use to transform themselves into change-makers and citizens of the world. Dr. Maria Montessori said it most eloquently:

> An education capable of saving humanity is no small undertaking; it involves the spiritual development of man, the enhancement of his value as an individual, and the preparation of young people to understand the times in which they live. (Montessori, 2004, p. 30)

Saving humanity? That does not seem simple at all!

Yet, it is the vision of both educator and parent to see that the child's talents, skills, and ambitions are developed to their fullest value and potential.

But, how in the world do we get there?

Together, with a carefully prepared emotional environment, a chrysalis, if you will.

So, where does the conversation begin?

It begins with a word of gratitude. Thank you to the parents, families, guardians and caregivers who share their children with educators in schools and educational settings around the globe; and to you, dear reader, for caring to build rapport with your child's teacher enough to pick this book. As a parent, your time is valuable, your demands are high and your energies are divided between home and workplace.

Chapter I: It Takes a Village

Children do not come into the world with a direction manual, there is not a "how to" video that guarantees success, there is no device that creates more time or resources to share with them and there is no article, meme or post that answers all your questions.

Fortunately, you have this book which is a collection of wisdom and suggestions I gathered during 30 years of working with children and parents and during candid conversations with more than 100 educators in public, private, Montessori, and traditional educational and childcare settings.

This book is intended to be a brief catalyst of thought and action. A place to begin to work together because even the strongest butterflies need a little help to make their environments and conditions as conducive as possible before their wings are spread to fly.

How This Book Works
(so you will not have to)

(Well, maybe some work, but I promise it is worth it!)

You are busy!

I know it!

This book has been written to be a quick read to respectfully convey ideas to those who are so important to children—You!

It is written to support the educators who serve children—Us!

It is written to honor the process through which children make tremendous gains—Together!

This book is written with respect to the intensive love and labor required to raise children by parents, extended family members, caregivers, and yes, even educators. Of course, families and caregivers have the greatest and longest impact in the lifetime of an individual, and I suspect you can conjure the

Chapter I: It Takes a Village

memory of your favorite or least favorite teacher with ease. The impact of educators is significant as well.

The topic of parent engagement is too important to miss sharing, but your time for reading a book may be brief. Therefore, I have included **an idea for consideration** at the end of many sections of this book. These are designed to summarize the section and can be your quick read on the topic. You may want to skim the entire book for a quick read and then revisit sections when time allows or if you are curious to know more.

As a Montessori teacher, I have learned that the rationale behind any action, or choice of words, is important. So, the words and intent for **an idea for consideration** is to provide adults raising children with suggestions that surfaced from surveys of educators who were asked to anonymously and candidly offer a suggestion for parents that would help support their work in the classroom. This book brings those most common topics to light for your examination.

Are you interested in further activity? As you wade through the ideas for consideration, you will find spaces within this book for your reflections on the topics. Mason and Reagan's mom asked, "What are my next steps?". I thought she asked a terrific question! So, you may want to use the spaces provided to jot down your reflections of the section or to program your active "next steps". You may also consider addressing the topics with your child's teacher and having a candid conversation with each other about the ideas.

Chapter I: It Takes a Village

I grew up in an old Victorian house in a small town on the east coast. I was a "town-ie". My hometown was predominantly rural dairy farms with a small downtown that was incorporated the same year my parent's house was built in 1860. My uncle lived across the street. My grandparents lived a block away between my home and my elementary school. I walked the two blocks to school from kindergarten until eighth grade and waved to my grandparents daily as I passed. I regularly hopped the three-foot chain-link fence that separated me from my neighbor, a friend of the same age, until her dad built us a gate—we still jumped the fence anyway. These people were my village—they were the extended family and friends who created the fabric of my early development. They guided when necessary and celebrated when occasions arose.

Now I live in a colorful Florida home in an ever-growing suburb outside a city of half a million people. I still travel to school, but by car. And my fence hopping days have passed, thank goodness because the fences in my neighborhood are six feet tall privacy fences!

I hear children behind those fences occasionally. I cannot see them, but I see the tops of their play structures. The children in my neighborhood ride to school in their parents' cars and sometimes travel great distances to see their extended family. Their village is different from mine, but their needs are the same—they require a diverse and deliberate group of people to shape their experiences and understanding of the world. They require friends, neighbors, families, and communities.

And they need parents and teachers working together, intentionally.

A family gathers and waits. Perhaps they have been waiting for nine months or perhaps they have been waiting for years for this moment. They may be in hospital waiting rooms, in adjacent rooms in homes, at adoption agencies, or miles away watching for the text announcement on their phone.

The soon to be new parents' emotions run from exaltation, to excitement, to apprehension, to "oh no, I'm not ready!"

But ready or not, here they come!

From the moment a child is placed in the arms of an anxiously awaiting parent, guardian or caregiver, that adult becomes the most important teacher in the life of that child. Some lessons are directly taught. Expectations about where to play safely, when to go to bed (hopefully) and what to eat (mostly) are shared with even the youngest children. Parents teach children about right and wrong, how to take care of themselves, and how to interact with others. Other instructions are less direct. Those indirect lessons convey beliefs, attitudes, judgments and biases towards self, others and situations—and can be as powerful in shaping the child's personality and behaviors as those moments when we share direct guidance.

Chapter I: It Takes a Village

Raising children is the most important, exhausting, joyful, challenging, and awe-inspiring privilege that can be shared with another human being. At times our hearts sing, and we believe we were meant to parent this incredible being in our care. At times our hearts break and we question every interaction we have with the child. It is in moments of both joy and grief when we look to our "village"—those people, organizations, books, websites, blogs, and teachers who support us in our metamorphosis into parents, guardians and caregivers.

There is a proverb that states, "It takes a village to raise a child." I believe there is tremendous sophistication in that folk wisdom. I have guided my teaching career with this belief:

> The pathway for global wellness lies in the spirit of children who deserve to be cared for by communities of adults with common goals and common purposes— raising healthy children. (Harman, 2018, p. 37)

The purpose of this book is to let those raising children know that they are not alone in their work. Teachers and caregivers are resources with education, experience and intentional strategies to assist in the process of raising children. It is, after all, what they do on a daily basis.

Parents and guardians are experts in their own professions, trust me, you do not want me to prepare your taxes, repair your garage door or build your computer! However, the knowledge and skills developed by teachers and caregivers center on children. Let us help you.

We live in a world where we seem to be divided by security measures, privacy fences and social media provocations. We have endured a global pandemic that has further divided us. Yet, it is within beautiful and imperfect communities where novices and experts come together to meet and support one another. Teachers and caregivers are an integral part of that community because they have intentionally chosen the education of children as their contribution to the "village".

Not to "Should" on You

You may wonder what a teacher has to share with parents about raising children. A colleague once told me, "There are just some things that teachers and grandparents know that maybe parents should know."

This book is not designed to "should" or "shouldn't" on parents, or to add more burdens to the tremendous responsibility of raising children. This book is designed to bring awareness to the dynamic opportunity that parents have when intentionally partnering with their children's teachers.

You may also wonder if your child's teacher is hoping to build a partnership with you. My advice is, "Ask. Don't be shy!" Your role is too important and your support is too necessary to let the opportunity pass.

I often tell my adult children, "If you do not ask, then the answer is 'no'". In my first book *Intentional Connections: A Practical Guide to Parent Engagement in the Early Childhood and Lower Elementary Classroom*, I give teachers some words to share with parents.

> Hello, I am (teacher's name). It is my goal to gain your confidence, entice, persuade, enlist, inspire and intentionally connect with you so we, together, can work toward the best possible educational outcome for your child. (Harman, 2018, p. 119)

I wish to share with you the same encouragement, and perhaps some similar words.

> Hello, I am (child's name)'s mom/dad/auntie/etc., and I would really like to build an intentionally connected partnership with you so we, together, can work toward the best possible educational outcome for my child.

If you get a surprised look from your child's teacher, you can share my book to get things started.

Why Parent and Teacher Engagement Matters

The subject line of the email read...

"Aubrey at school"... And her parents thought, "Oh no! What has she done?"

"Tyson at school"... And his grandma thought, "I only hear from his teacher when he's in trouble."

"Jonna at school"... And her auntie thought, "I don't have time for one more thing."

Have you ever received a "Johnny at school" email? They elicit an immediate emotional response when discovered by a parent in an email inbox. Perhaps the reaction is more of a result of the relationship between the adults than the actions of the child. After all, we live in a time when we are divided by a number of factors—race, gender, political views, to name only a few, but what if we focus upon the very thing that unites us?—children! Children are honest, expressive and direct. They ask, "Do you want to play?", "Will you be my friend?" and they form relationships. I tried this direct approach with my friend, Resa Steindel Brown, author of *The Call to Brilliance*. We began a conversation about a business transaction that resulted in a number of email exchanges. I boldly asked, "Will you be my friend." Guess what? It worked, we are friends!

Perhaps we could utilize the wisdom of children in relationships between parents and teachers. How powerful is it for young children to see, hear and feel parents and teachers in roles as collaborators, partners and, perhaps, friends. Imagine the impact of an intentional collaboration between adults instead of a random placement of a child with a teacher where a relationship is assumed to develop. Imagine the potential of a group of adults in partnership for the prosperity of a child.

Imagine the possibilities of a child who is aware of adults who believe in them.

The greatest indicator of a child's success at school is not the financial or social status of the family, but the partnership and engagement of parents and teachers with one another. (Henderson and Berla, 1994) (Kalina and Stehu, 2010). Partnerships create common expectations, common language and demonstrate to the child that the adults in their life are working together for their good and are creating a "village" of care and support.

My advice to parents and teachers alike is to remember the phrase, "Will you help me help them?". It is direct and focuses attention not on the issues that can divide adults, but focuses attention on a common investment—a child.

Childhood as Observed by Dr. Maria Montessori

Most of my professional experience has been spent in Montessori settings so I often turn to the writings of Dr. Maria Montessori for guidance. Her immense contribution to education was based on her intensive scientific observation of children. Children have needs, perceptions and gifts that are dramatically different than adults', and they need supportive adults from a variety of settings including home and school. Some contemporary experts in child development call this an

Chapter I: It Takes a Village

"ecological" perspective of support whereby the adults from all areas of the child's life are impactful.

We know that children are not simply little adults. Their needs and behaviors are strikingly different from our own. One concept that demonstrates the vast differences between adults and children is the concept of work. It is often said that play is the work of the child and indeed that is true. However, play and work for children is one in the same, while adult understanding of the concept is quite different. I have observed plenty of children deeply and joyfully concentrating for a long period of time while sweeping the floor with a dustpan and brush. However, you and I would complete the task in a brief moment and would find little satisfaction in the task. Dr. Montessori said:

> A child is always busy working on his own development. When a grown-up thinks of work, he thinks of doing something as a means to an end—spending his days in an office for the sake of a salary—but a child's work is based on doing things for their own sake. (Montessori, 2017, p. 18)

Children work, play and achieve in an emotional environment created by adults in partnership. We have an enormous opportunity to create an atmosphere of stable support which promotes emotional well-being between home and school.

If you could ask a child where they would rather work, they would tell you in a collaborative environment where their interests are protected and encouraged by caring adults. Of course, the child cannot explain this need. In *The Child, Society and the World,* Dr. Montessori writes the "principle of their own growth, they cannot possibly explain to anyone." (Montessori, 2016, p. 4)

Dr. Montessori continues:

They are full of knowledge. This would seem to be a contradiction, but the truth is that these children must take knowledge by themselves from the environment. (Montessori, 2016, p. 44)

This environment, dear parents, guardians and caregivers, includes us!

Some Parenting Basics

Children are not the only individuals on a developmental journey. You are on that journey, too! When you reflect on the growth you have experienced with your children, you may see that there is a wealth of knowledge you have acquired. According to author and researcher, Ellen Galinsky, parents experience six growth paths that correspond to the development of the children they are parenting.

The first occurs before the child arrives. It is called "image making" during which time parents prepare for the child's arrival and conjure images of who the child will be and what the child will do as they grow.

The second stage called "nurturing" occurs from the child's birth through the second year. This stage ushers in a deep bonding with the child and an adjustment to lifestyle. I am pretty sure parents do not fantasize about 3 am feedings or toddlers who discover the word "no"!

The third stage is coined as the period of "authority" and is the time that parents spend energy helping children develop patterns of behavior. It occurs from age 2 through 6. In Montessori, we refer to this activity of guiding children's behavior as Grace and Courtesy, during which time children are taught how to care for themselves, others and their environment. Parents can use this period of time to lean into relationships with other primary caregivers, including their teachers!

The fourth stage is referred to as the "interpretive" stage and occurs from 6 to 12 years of age. Among a great many skills taught during this time, parents are guiding children in forming and interpreting social experiences outside of the home. The lessons of Grace and Courtesy extend beyond the walls of their schools as children are capable of imagining the possibilities in social, emotional, cognitive and physical realms. Parents often feel a heart tug as children attend slumber parties with best friends and peers who are of deep importance to the child.

The fifth stage is the period of "interdependence" and occurs from age 12 to 18. These are the tumultuous teen years. The theme of control appears again as children this age face greater challenges in decision-making with skills that flow between reason and emotion. Often parents report this period as a time during which they feel least prepared. The images held from infancy may need revision as the teen alters between distance and closeness, and separateness and connectedness with the parent.

The sixth stage occurs between 18 and 24 years and is called "departure". Perhaps you felt a rock in your gut as you read the words. The child departs to make their own way in the world. They choose work, career and relationship paths. The relationship with the parent is ultimately redefined. New ways of being together emerge and it often compels parents to reflect on their successes and failures throughout the child's development. Galinsky notes: "In accepting this separate identity, parents learn that to accept separateness implies the beginning of a new connection." (Galinsky, 1989, p.4)

As a mother of adult children, I can comfortably attest that the journey does not end there. Parents and caregivers celebrate and mourn with their children throughout a lifetime of experiences. It is a tremendous responsibility and a deep honor to parent a child and you do not need to do it alone! There are experienced experts to help you along the way—they are called your children's teachers.

Chapter II: The Relationship Between Adults: Fostering Community

"The best way to find out if you can trust somebody is to trust them."

—Ernest Hemingway

Trust

The Hemingway quote is easier said than done when it comes to building trust in relationships. When my cell phone displays "potential spam" during a call my tendency to mistrust is strong; I do not answer the call. People, however, do not have displays that read "potential spam" or "trustworthy". The decision to trust or mistrust someone in real life is much more complex. Yet, every relationship website, meme and advice article, suggests trust is an important indicator of the quality of the relationship.

Trust is critical in the relationship between teachers and parents. Many educators had positive school experiences as children. School may have been a place of success, safety or enjoyment and those experiences made returning a comfortable place for building a career. Perhaps, as an adult, you may look back on your childhood and youth and have some of those same positive feelings. However, unlike teachers, you chose other occupations. Meanwhile, some adults have unfavorable memories of school experiences for a myriad of reasons and school is not a place of joyful memories or trust.

Regardless of the adults' experiences, sometimes we have to accept Hemingway's advice and trust one another. For adults with positive school memories the idea of trusting may come naturally. For others, an intentional choice to trust a teacher is a powerful decision that will benefit your child. Ultimately, it is as Hemingway and I suggest, one must make the decision to be trusting and to be trustworthy.

But how do teachers and parents develop trust in one another once the decision is made to do so? According to provisional psychologist Heather Craig, here are ways trust is built:

- keeping your word
- careful decision-making
- being consistent
- acknowledging that trust takes time to develop
- being honest
- admitting when you are wrong
- sharing your feelings
- showing kindness
- being open for participation and communication (Craig, 2022)

Wow! That is a lengthy menu of behaviors that lead to trust. So, maybe we can approach one thing at a time. How about we begin with kindness? My mother used to share folk advice. As a child I thought it was "uncool", but now I see the beauty in her wisdom. She would tell me, "You'll catch more flies with honey than vinegar." I wondered why we wanted to catch flies—perhaps it was because I grew up near dairy farms? Now I understand it was about kindness. It was about making an intentional choice to be kind. Kindness is easy to implement and it is a powerful example to demonstrate for your child.

And be gentle with yourself—you are developing as a parent and may not "do it" perfectly every time, but you are valued nonetheless. (This is a little of my folk wisdom.)

An Idea for Consideration

Build a relationship with the professional that is aiding your child's development. Trust their training, education, and experience.

Reflections:

Next Steps:

Discussions with my child's teachers:

Communication

"If the person you are talking to does not appear to be listening, be patient. It may simply be that he has a small piece of fluff in his ear."

—Winnie the Pooh, A. A. Milne

Pooh bear was right, communication is about talking and listening. One of the many lessons taught by the pandemic, especially during lockdown, was that communication between teachers, parents and caregivers was crucial for the success of the child in distance-learning settings. It certainly required patience.

Communication is the foundation upon which nearly all interactions between school and home are based. This became dramatically evident during the spring of 2020 when families and teachers pivoted to remote learning and suddenly, we were interacting in unfamiliar ways. School closures and the lack of physical proximity created challenges for many teachers and families, but those who had consciously practiced school and home communication throughout the year found that that was a little less of a hurdle. The intentional relationships built prior to the closure helped many who felt scared, confused, isolated and unsure. In many cases, parents learned about the significance of their role in their child's education. Parents, teachers, and school personnel did the best they could in a situation that they could never have imagined previously.

Teachers learned that there are a wealth of tools and apps that are designed with the purpose of developing communication between schools and families. Chances are, many of those tools have continued to be used to share pictures, videos, classroom messages and school updates.

However, there are times when even the best attempts at communication are ineffective. Sometimes our inboxes are so full with correspondence that it is difficult to decipher the important information from the less important information, the "right now" from "do it later" messages, and the information that is relevant to the individual from the message that is intended for the group. More information is not necessarily effectively delivered information.

In *Intentional Connections*, I suggest communications that move from the school to the home be delivered consistently at the same time and on the same day. A Friday newsletter delivered at 3:00pm or a Monday school update that hits inboxes at 9:00am is easier to anticipate than information that is delivered randomly throughout the week.

I also encourage brevity. There is a deliberate purpose behind the length of this booklet. I respect your time.

Telling your child's teacher how you are most likely to interact, respond to, or read information helps them determine the best methods of delivery. However, the best planned communication from school is only effective when families read and pay attention to the information—that part is your responsibility. Communication works best when we all remove the "fluff" from our ears.

Receiving information is only a part of the communication formula, however. Sharing information with schools and teachers is also crucial and can solidify the parent-teacher relationship. Some items for reflection are:

- Do I know how to give and receive information to my child's teacher?
- Can I commit to reading communications?
- Do I feel comfortable communicating with my child's teacher?
- Can I share ideas?
- Do I go directly to the teacher when the need arises?
- Do I avoid school gossip, especially on social media?
- Do I have a voice in my child's school or care situation?

- Do I know how to address school or classroom concerns and celebrations?
- Do I attend parent teacher conferences and/or other events?
- Do I have a role in decision-making?
- Am I able and willing to engage with my child's school?

An Idea for Consideration

Take time to give and receive information and go directly to the source when necessary.

Reflections:

Next Steps:

Discussions with my child's teachers:

Be ~~Involved~~, Better Yet...Be Engaged

"Try to be a rainbow in someone's cloud"

—Maya Angelou

Despite their common appearance on pages of children's artwork, rainbows do not just happen. There are some necessary conditions that must occur for a rainbow to appear. A rainbow occurs when a cloud, raindrops and the sun are engaged with one another.

The strikethrough above is not a typo that was missed in editing; it is intentional. I chose the word "engaged" specifically in the scenario because engagement implies "with" one another and coming together, while involved implies "doing to". So, when teachers and families are involved with one another, it may sound like a greeting at drop-off or pick-up. It may look like an email explaining a school procedure or a reason for an absence.

However, engagement takes the relationship deeper; it looks like smiles and jubilance when growth is celebrated. It sounds like a brainstorming conversation between a teacher and parent when addressing a challenge together, and it may feel like parallel joy and heartbreak.

During their career hundreds, maybe even thousands of children will cross the threshold into their teacher's classroom. Each child will bring their unique personalities, individual needs, and dreams into that room.

But at 3:30 or so each day, teachers return them to their parents. Those same personalities, needs and dreams appear on their parent's threshold.

It seems evident to me that we are raising a child together. Whether we acknowledge it as such or not, we are on a journey together, witnessing the child learn and grow. What if we do see one another as a resource? Your knowledge of the child is much deeper than ours. We have education, training and experience with hundreds of children and families. What if we intentionally engage "with" one another for the child's benefit?

The research suggests the child will conclude that their support system is one of collaboration and commitment, and the partnership we develop for your child will be meaningful and impactful. Our goal is common, to "guide" the child!

And who knows, we may both end up with pictures of rainbows for our refrigerators!

An Idea for Consideration

"Don't be shy!" If your child's teacher has not explicitly discussed what engagement looks like, just ask! If they have not thought of it before perhaps you can recommend an author!

Reflections:

Next Steps:

Discussions with my child's teachers:

Chapter III: The Relationship with the Child: Fostering Growth

"We can love our children so dearly that it makes us blind to what is best for them. We can desire so eagerly that they shall grow into fine men and women that we correct and frustrate them at every turn without realizing that they have within themselves the power of their own development."

— Maria Montessori, 2017, p. 13

Autonomy

Long before my daughter Alicia could speak, there were the elbows! The elbows that jutted outward, sometimes accompanied with a slight spin that silently spoke, "I can do it myself!". Then spoken language appeared— "Me do it!" It was often accompanied by the elbow body language, and was clearly a statement expressing her desire and need to explore and interact with her environment independently and without interference.

Sometimes the cry of independence occurs at the most difficult times. Perhaps you are trying to leave the house and a young child insists on putting on their own shoes. At other times, you are in a public setting like the grocery store and your preschooler insists on pushing the cart. The same call for autonomy reappears intensely during adolescence.

The human tendency for autonomy, independence and self-determination exists throughout a lifetime. It is pronounced loudly in toddlers, adolescents and fiercely independent adults who exclaim or act upon variations of, "you're not the boss of me!"

So why is all of this energy devoted to developing autonomy? When a child is born, they are completely dependent upon their caregivers. Human babies do not have the ability to stand, walk, run, forage for food or many of the other independent behaviors that are typical for other animal babies.

Human development is much slower and requires more care, but the movement towards independence begins as soon as the human infant starts to move. Sometimes movements towards independence are met with moments of celebration, for instance, when a child takes their first steps or uses the toilet. Other independent activities challenge the precious time that parents and caregivers have when trying to get to work and school each morning. Children may have their own ideas about the contents of their lunchboxes or the clothes they will wear. Contrary to the emotions adults may feel, those moments of demanding independence are necessary for the development of the child and are not just an attempt to drive you bananas.

Consider giving yourself five deep breaths to get through those feelings of frustration, because independence is one of the most powerful skills you can help your child develop.

Self-confidence, motivation, self-reliance, competence, internal discipline, problem-solving, decision-making, and responsibility are some of the natural by-products of fostering independence in children. Whereas lack of faith in oneself and learned helplessness can be attitudes developed when children

Chapter III: The Relationship with the Child: Fostering Growth

are not given opportunities to do things for themselves, or are not provided with control over some of their choices.

The conditions and opportunities created by adults to encourage independence in children could also include establishing routines. For example, bedtime could be a routine of taking a bath, choosing between two sets of pajamas, brushing teeth and choosing a book (Would you like this picture book or a chapter from a chapter book?), a hug and a kiss, and then lights out. It may seem like a big production just to ensure adequate rest, but routines satisfy the young child's need for order. Knowing what to expect next helps children move through routines smoothly and independently.

Choice can be a beneficial strategy to implement during the challenging moments. Providing children with some degree of choice may eliminate struggles and, more importantly, they encourage the child to exercise independence within a prepared environment that adults create.

Pre-teaching is a powerful tool used by early childhood educators to help children prepare for moments that are out of the ordinary and not routine, like field trips or classroom visitors. For parents and caregivers, those moments are plentiful when activities take the child out of the home.

Pre-teaching may sound like, "We are going to the grocery store. You may choose one item to put in the cart. So, you have to decide which is the one item you would like the most."

It may also sound like, "When we go to the soccer game today, I expect you to be okay if you do not get to play first. Let's practice taking three deep breaths to calm your body in case you need to use it if you are feeling disappointed."

Pre-teaching will allow you to be proactive instead of reactive and will allow your child to develop autonomous control over their own actions.

An Idea for Consideration

Allow children to exercise independence through choice by providing options, routines and pre-teaching.

Reflections:

Next Steps:

Discussions with my child's teacher:

Accountability

"...with great power comes great responsibility"

— Benjamin Parker to Peter Parker (Spiderman)

"She started it!" "He did it first!" "They made me do it!" These are some of the classic childhood deflections of responsibility for one's own actions and reactions. Oddly, sometimes we hear these immature responses coming from adults as well with slightly more sophisticated language, of course.

Accountability means accepting the consequences for one's behavior and has the word "able" as part of its root. It does *not* mean mistakes do not happen.

Actually, in many cases learning occurs more powerfully, and we become able when mistakes do happen. How we learn from mistakes has a great deal to do with the separation of judgment and shame from the error. For example, we can address the common childhood activity of spilling. A child who feels shame about spilling cereal may blame someone else for the spill. This is an opportunity to tell the child that spills happen and it is okay when they do. Adults can say, "We simply clean up the spill. May I show you how to use the dustpan and brush?" The next time a spill occurs, (and they will) the child will reach for the tools to remedy the overturned items. Please note the child, not the adult, cleaned up the spill in the above scenario and took full responsibility for the actions while learning how to use a dustpan and brush. The mistake is "no big deal" and can be corrected.

Sometimes, errors are "big deals", like when a child hurts another child. In regards to pre-teaching. I have found strategies that start with only 2 rules are easiest. Of course, these rules are unique to each home and situation. Here are some common themes and general ideas:

- We do not hurt ourselves or others.
- We are not disruptive.
- We knock on doors before entering.
- We clean up after ourselves.
- We tell the truth.
- Be a good role model.
- Own your mistakes.

The rules could go on and on depending upon the age of your child, a situation that has currently arisen and your style of parenting. Psychotherapist, Amy Morin, suggests five common structures of rules for living with children. Her suggestions for types of rules are based around safety, morality, healthy habits, social skills and preparation for the real world.

As a public school Montessori educator, I was trained in an approach to trauma-informed care known as Behavior Intervention Support Team (BIST), designed by Cornerstones of Care. Initially, I was unsure about the compatibility between this strategy and my Montessori methods and ideologies. However, I soon adopted the two-rule approach in my early childhood environment as delivered through the training. The first two rules listed above were the rules of my school. "We can't be hurtful." and "We can't be disruptive." I soon found when speaking with children who required redirection that all of the behaviors that required redirection fell within these two rules. I could say to a child, "Oops, I noticed you forgot one of our rules that we can't be hurtful or we can't be disruptive. Which one did you forget?" Even the youngest 3 year-old in my class began to identify their mistake or missing skill and accept accountability without shame or blame. The teachable moment continued with questions such as:

- "What could you do differently?"
- "Let's practice your new idea, do you want to practice once or two times?"

I found this strategy extremely helpful, especially when parents and I were using the same language at home and at school. It proved beneficial to the child since the expectations and the language were clear and simple to navigate when the rules were limited to one or the other.

Redirection of behavioral choices are opportunities for learning and are a significant responsibility of parenting a child. However, the goal of discipline is for it to become an inner process wherein individuals try to make their best judgments and if they make a mistake, they accept the error and try something differently, not because there are rules, but because it feels good to do the right thing for oneself and others and grow. And it certainly requires much less energy than, "She started it!" "He did it first!" and "They made me do it!" In *The Absorbent Mind*, Dr. Montessori wrote,

> Conscious will is a power which develops with use and activity. We must aim at cultivating the will, not at breaking it. (Montessori, 1995, p. 254)

An Idea for Consideration

Adopt the idea that behavior regulation is a learning opportunity for children to develop social skills.

Reflections:

Next Steps:

Discussions with my child's teachers:

Intellectual Development

Most teachers enter into the field of education to help children and parents with much more than reading, writing and arithmetic. Dr. Montessori referred to education as "a help to life" (Montessori, 2018, p. 38) not only the acquisition of academic and school-related skills. Intellectual development is about the journey toward knowledge, curiosity, and creativity, not just the acquisition of skills required to pass a standardized test.

She also wrote:

> The urge towards growth lies within the child himself—his intelligence and character will grow whatever we may do, but we can help or hinder the growth. (Montessori, 2018, p. 48)

Adults, and especially parents and primary caregivers, are the most important teachers in a child's life. When children are read to and see adults reading books, they develop a love of reading. When they hear, "I'm terrible at math," they adopt those feelings as well. When they receive a written note in their lunchbox, inbox, or mailbox, they learn that the written word is a powerful tool that can build others up or devastate feelings. When we demonstrate kindness, they learn to express kindness. The human factor of a child's surroundings cannot be underestimated. For children age 3 to 6, the absorbent mind is taking in impressions from the environment without filtration. So, how does this affect intellectual development?

Our actions and words provide lessons to children at all times and in all settings, not just at school. As adults we may want to ask ourselves, "Is this behavior/value/attitude/lesson what I wish to impart upon my child?"

As the child's first and most important teacher, teach by example; encourage independence: encourage positive attitudes toward learning and school: build trusting, open, supportive relationships with those providing care for your child outside your home; remove obstacles that inhibit growth; allow time for children to construct their learning, and value all types of learning.

As a Montessori educator I was trained to focus upon development of the "whole child". This includes emotional development, social development, physical development and cognitive development. It means that the environments where

Chapter III: The Relationship with the Child: Fostering Growth

children spend their days should be safe, healthy, supporting, engaging and challenging. However, as a teacher I was never alone. Partnerships with parents and primary caregivers were essential for the best outcomes of my students.

When supporting your child's intellectual development at home, follow the teacher's guidance, ask questions, and trust the reasons you are being asked to do something.

Some great ways to help your children develop intellectual abilities are to:

- Read to your child daily. (Often bedtime stories are a favorite.)

- Provide tools to practice writing. (Did you know manipulating dough helps children strengthen writing skills?)

- Make numbers a regular part of conversation and experiences, such as "your brother, your grandmother, you and I can each have one fourth of this orange", "Can you push "one-hundred fifteen on the microwave to cook our oatmeal?" or "Let's all dance for one minute, freeze for one minute, then dance again for another minute."

- In my personal mantra, "Have fun. Learn lots. Make new friends." —fun and learning are two-thirds of the formula. (See how I threw some math language in there?) Learning and fun can, and often do, accompany one another.

- Working on a puzzle together strengthens children's visual skills and is fun. Collecting rocks while observing birds flying overhead when on a walk from the car to the school building can provide classification skills of non-living and living things in the child's environment, which can help build vocabulary.

Building vocabulary is probably the most natural and easiest activity that develops your child's intellectual skills. Read, read, read and talk, talk, talk with your child! Maybe learn some new vocabulary together. Learn a new language together. Collect words: What is the name of a male hawk? What is the name of a female hawk? What is a baby hawk called? What is the name for a group of hawks? (A quick internet search yields a tierces, hen, eya and kettle to answer the questions above!)

Model asking questions about a word's meaning. This happens frequently when my husband talks about computer programming at our house. This type of modeling also demonstrates that learning is a lifelong pursuit and a "help to life" that occurs within and outside of our formal places of learning.

An Idea for Consideration

Embrace your role as your child's first and most important teacher!

Reflections:

Next Steps:

Discussions with my child's teachers:

Chapter IV: The Relationship with the Environment: Removing Obstacles

"…unless we adults are enlightened, either by nature or science, as to the way in which his mind develops, we are likely to become the greatest obstacles to his progress."

— Maria Montessori, 1995, p. 166

An obstacle is something that restricts, blocks, hinders, or impedes, progress. It can be as obvious as a detour sign or as subtle as an eye-roll. They can be as short-lived as a reboot on your computer or as long-lasting as a phobia. However, most caregivers, parents and teachers would agree that obstacles are a part of the human experience and not something for which we wish to be responsible, especially when it impacts a child's development.

Discretion: Little Pitchers, Big Ears

Most of us can remember with awe and enthusiasm when our children were learning to talk. The wonderful sound of "da-da" or "ma-ma" was met with sheer joy as we realized the means through which we could communicate with our children was developing into a spoken language. It is effortless for the typical developing child. Dr. Maria Montessori referred to this time of development as the period of the absorbent mind. She asked:

> How does it happen that the child learns to speak? How is it that, among the thousands of sounds and noises that surround him, he...reproduces only those of the human voice? (Montessori, 1995, p. 24)

Montessorian and author, Aline Wolf, reminds us "He does not go around ringing like the telephone or barking like a dog." (2005, p. 8) And we say thank goodness! The chatter and questions are often enough at the end of a parent's busy work day, the last thing needed is a barking child added to the din!

As easily as a child develops speech by absorbing language, they can absorb attitudes as well. We often assume children are busy playing or are engrossed in some activity, but the absorbent mind attends to our voices more than any stimulation provided by a toy. Our conversations speak volumes to children about our feelings—everything from something as simple as snack choices to complex issues like crises in the world. Our non-verbal communication also can broadcast our opinions with as much volume as our voices. The absorbent mind does not shut down like a child's toy, it is constantly taking in information from its environment, and there is no greater stimulus than a child's parent.

You may ask, "What does this have to do with relationships between parents, children and teachers?" It has a tremendous amount to do with these relationships since conversations and body language in the home influence the child's attitude toward school and their teacher. This does not mean conversations about school must be dripping with sweetness and agreement, but it does mean that conversations that express concern or disagreement are less impactful on our

Chapter IV: The Relationship with the Environment: Removing Obstacles

child's attitudes when they occur outside of the child's listening environment.

My husband would remark, "little pitchers have big ears" when our conversations were ones that we should not have within earshot of our children. It is an old-fashioned saying, but its meaning is still relevant today. Children adopt the attitudes of their homes and schools without intention and, sometimes without understanding. Political rhetoric provides a great example of the acquisition of ideas that children carry into schools from external sources. In recent history, debates concerning the character of political candidates have made their way into early childhood classrooms as children passionately proclaim a candidate's "goodness" or "badness" without any understanding of the complexity of political races or vast components of personality. These opinions are not a result of study of political science, but are a result of the absorbent mind.

Of course, disagreement is a natural component of any relationship. Just as any number of individuals can have multiple perspectives of a common occurrence, so too can parents and teachers have differing ideas about a child's development, achievement, and behaviors. These differences can provide opportunities for greater understanding for both teachers and parents and can be for the benefit of the child. However, children that are exposed to these differences in ideas may conclude and generalize that these environments that mean the most to them (home and school) and those who dwell there, are either "good" or "bad". This over-simplification and conclusion could create an obstacle that influences a child's attitude toward school, their abilities, and their trust.

An Idea for Consideration

Refrain from discussing negative school and teacher matters when children are present.

Reflections:

Next Steps:

Discussions with my child's teachers:

"We limit how much technology our kids use at home"

–Steve Jobs

Technology

Love it or hate it, technology is a constant presence in our lives, purses, and pockets. Devices put the world at our fingertips. They connect us with family, friends, and information from around the globe. They advance our sciences in ways we could not imagine only a few years ago. And on some occasions, devices can be a tremendous hindrance to young children's development because they interfere with the natural learning processes children experience.

Once, my husband and I went to dinner at a casual restaurant. I quickly noticed the young family and grandparents that arrived and were seated at the table next to us. I estimated the children to be 4 and 6 years old. They all talked and laughed as their server showed them to their table. However, once seated, the children ceased conversation. In each of their small hands was a tablet wrapped in the brightly-colored, thick

Chapter IV: The Relationship with the Environment: Removing Obstacles

protective cases. The adults continued to chat with one another and the grandfather tried to engage the children. He asked them about school, their friends and other topics, but to no avail.

He changed his approach to ask questions about the games the children were playing. He was met with silence and occasional "yeahs" and "uh-huhs", but clearly the opportunity for a brightly-colored, protective, multi-generational dinner and conversation was thwarted by the distraction caused by the tech devices. It saddened my heart, not because the device itself was hurting the child, but because the delight once demonstrated in the children's animated chatter with their grandfather ceased. The grandfather observed it as well. Eventually, he simply watched silently as the boys played the game on their tablets in the brightly-colored thick protective case.

On another occasion, I observed quite the opposite obstruction caused by a device. This time the device was in the hands of a distracted mother whose small daughter attempted to engage her in conversation. The child made statements and asked questions that the mother simply echoed back to the child. "I like this chicken dinner" the child stated and it was met with a distracted, "You like the chicken" with a brief glimpse over the top of a glitter encased cell phone.

Are we all guilty of distraction by devices? Yes, myself included. Emails demand our attention, questions are answered by search engines, games are rated by their addictiveness, and social media can entertain and make us feel connected and "liked". However, young children develop their social skills by imitating the adults in their environments and through the experience of interacting with others. Nothing can replace human contact. As stated in the previous section, children are drawn to the human voice. Regardless of the addictive potential of any device, a child will not learn to beep and whistle like a video game, but they will learn by engaging with the people in their lives. It is an opportunity we really do not want to miss.

But, you may ask, can technology make us smarter? Can it help make our work easier and is it important for education? My answer is yes, but the most advanced technology for the young child is their hands. Dr. Montessori wrote of the hand as "the companion of the mind" (Montessori, 1995, p. 151) She spoke of the hand in her lectures and in her writings that were based upon her scientific observations of developing children. She wrote of the hands as the tools for developing order and coordination that leads to concentration and ultimately independence in task and in expression.

There are no technological simulations that can replace the sight, sounds, scents, textures and tastes of a warm rain on our face; the campfire smell of toasted marshmallows; a grandma's warm embrace, or a plunge into a freshly raked pile of leaves.

These pleasures are for the hands and the senses to experience, to process, to internalize, and they convey information to all of the parts of the child much like the central processing unit does with our devices. Dr. Montessori wrote:

> The human hand, so delicate and so complicated, not only allows the mind to reveal itself but it enables the whole being to enter into special relationships with its environment. (Montessori, 1966, p. 81)

We would not dream of expecting our puppies to learn about "dog-ness" through online videos and interactive apps. That would be absurd! Dog owners enjoy the sniffs, licks, head tilts, and pounces of pups. Children require these opportunities to interact with their environments as well, including a little pouncing. Simply put, children learn by doing. Their hands are the devices they use to construct their knowledge about the world around them and the world within them.

An Idea for Consideration

Limit or eliminate the use of technology devices for young children, and offer children opportunities to practice social skills or explore the environment through hands-on learning.

Reflections:

Next Steps:

Discussions with my child's teachers:

"Grown-ups think of play as a purposeless occupation that keeps children happy and out of mischief, but actually when children are left to play by themselves very little of their activity is purposeless."

— Maria Montessori, 2017, p. 17

Play

One of my fondest memories of my son's childhood was what family lore refers to as "the summer of the quest for the queen ant". I know it sounds like the title of a bad sci-fi movie—it was actually the glorious adventure of a small boy, a stick and, what seemed like weeks of summertime play and bliss. It began with a child's wading pool on a lawn that I was trying to nurture into a lush, green suburban showpiece. I weeded, seeded and pampered it with the best novice gardening skills I could and then came the wading pool. Well, it did not take long before the patch of lawn was matted, thinning and, finally, a scarred piece of barren earth in the shape of a discount store, plastic, circular child's wading pool! So much for my trophy lawn and the plastic pool, for they both were abandoned when the "quest" and the true prize began. The first development was a simple anthill that quickly became two and then more. Next came the hours of observation, what Dr. Montessori referred to as the "contemplation of minute things" (1966, p. 68) Then the pivotal suggestion from my husband, "Ya know, there might be a queen ant under those ant hills!"

The work of the hand was assisted by sticks, shovels, bits of string, and an imagination ablaze with the possibility of locating the queen ant, that by the way, was never found.

The queen ant's location was never really the point of the "quest," for the play was the "work to create the man he will be" (Montessori, 2017, p. 44) Dr. Montessori reminds us of the vast differences between the adult, who produces through work, and the child who is not concerned with the purpose of his activity, but in the "doing" of the activity. She referred to play as the genuine work of the child. Play, not a dismissive activity, but the work the child uses to joyfully construct their understanding of themselves, others and the world around them.

Tremendous opportunities for growth occur when children are free to choose their play activity without scripted play themes generated by movies, games, video games or books. The deep play ideas or schemes, however, take time for the child to develop and deserve uninterrupted opportunities, as all good stories and projects do. In a Montessori setting, this uninterrupted time is typically 2-3 hours in length and allows the child to become truly immersed in the activity without distraction. Perhaps, undisturbed play of this suggested length is a luxury that busy families cannot afford. Perhaps, children who have not experienced long periods of play will find it difficult to entertain themselves. However, just as stamina is developed through exercise, stamina is also developed through practice and opportunities, so start with shorter periods of play until a time of greater length is appropriate.

Early childhood was formerly the period of play, but academic preschools and kindergartens, organized sports and intrusions in our homes in the form of streaming videos, television, and video games defraud children of the joy of boats made of cardboard boxes, forts constructed of blankets, fairy rings fabricated out of rocks in the yard and sticks that may be the tool that finds the elusive queen ant.

This is not to say that children's play should never be interrupted by the reality of scheduling such as work, school or social opportunities; instead, it is to suggest that children benefit from unscheduled and uninterrupted playtime, even if that unscheduled time must be planned and intentionally reserved. Perhaps, think of this gift of time as an appointment, much like soccer practice and music lessons, but without a commute! You may find that the gift of scheduled playtime for grown-ups may be beneficial for the adults who care for young children as well. After all, the joy of playtime has no age limit!

An Idea for Consideration

Allow for uninterrupted play time with toys or materials that allow for construction and imaginary play.

Reflections:

Next Steps:

Discussions with my child's teachers:

Chapter V: Partnership: A Word of Appreciation

What an amazing journey a child makes from conception to adulthood. The conditions had to be just right for cells to form and develop; for birth to occur; for development during childhood to take place; for survival of the trials of adulthood to transpire; for the presence of a life on a beautiful planet to occur, and to exist in a vast universe. It staggers my mind to consider, "What are the odds of me?".

None of us got here alone. We were dependent upon the environments that surrounded us, including the people. It is a journey nothing short of a miracle.

The same is true of our children, they are on an incredible journey and we are privileged to accompany them. However, we do not need to do it alone. Our combined efforts aid children as they construct their learning and meaning from the environments we prepare intentionally. Our intentional connections with one another provide support for the child during difficulties, provide a witness for celebrations, and provide a deliberate environment wherein we try to contribute to the unfurling of the child's "wings".

The poet Kahlil Gibran (1883-1931) said it most beautifully in *The Prophet*:

On Children

And a woman who held a babe against her bosom said, Speak to us of children.

And he said:

Your children are not your children.

They are the sons and daughters of Life's longing for itself.

They come through you but not from you,

And though they are with you yet they belong not to you.

You may give them your love but not your thoughts,

For they have their own thoughts.

You may house their bodies but not their souls,

For their souls dwell in the house of tomorrow, which you cannot visit, not even in your dreams.

You may strive to be like them, but seek not to make them like you.

For life goes not backward nor tarries with yesterday.

You are the bows from which your children as living arrows are sent forth.

The archer sees the mark upon the path of the infinite, and He bends you with His might that His arrows may go swift and far.

Let your bending in the archer's hand be for gladness;

For even as He loves the arrow that flies, so He loves also the bow that is stable.

(Gibran, 2020)

Gibran claims his words were, "a part of me" for years. Similarly, children and their families are a part of me and every other teacher. And we are a part of your family. The intricacies of our relationships are complex, but at times, laced with laughter. They are challenging, enriching and always interwoven with opportunities to learn. They are connections that link us in relationships that make a difference in the lives of those children. We are the stable bow and the nurturing chrysalis from which they can fly.

An Idea for Consideration

Practice gratitude.

References

Adams, K. S., & Christenson, S. L. (2000). *Trust and the Family–School Relationship Examination of Parent–Teacher Differences in Elementary and Secondary Grades*. Journal of School Psychology, *38*(5), 477–497. https://doi.org/10.1016/s0022-4405(00)00048-0

Behavior intervention support team (BIST). Behavior Intervention Support Team (BIST) " BIST. (n.d.). Retrieved September 27, 2021, from https://bist.org/

Corrigan, M. W., & Chapman, P. E. (n.d.). *Radical Pedagogy (2008)*. Trust in teachers: a motivating element to learning. Retrieved November 14, 2021, from https://radicalpedagogy.icaap.org/content/issue9_2/Corrigan_Chapman.html

Craig, H. (2022, June 4). *10 Ways to Build Trust In a Relationship*. PositivePsychology.com. Retrieved June 10, 2022, from https://positivepsychology.com/build-trust/

Gibran, K. (2020). On Children. In *The Prophet*. poem, READ & CO Books.

Galinsky, E. (1989). *The six stages of parenthood*. Addison-Wesley. Henderson, A., & Berla, N. (1997). *A New Generation of Evidence: The Family is Critical to Student Achievement*. Amazon. Retrieved October 12, 2021, from https://www.amazon.com/New-Generation-Evidence-Critical-Achievement/dp/0934460418

Kalin, J., & Šteh, B. (2010, May 6). *Advantages and Conditions for Effective Teacher-Parent Co-Operation*. Procedia - Social and Behavioral Sciences. Retrieved September 18, 2021, from https://www.sciencedirect.com/science/article/pii/S1877042810008360

Montessori, M. (1966). *The Secret of Childhood.* New York: Ballantine Books.

Montessori, M. (1995). *The Absorbent Mind.* New York: Henry Holt and Company.

Montessori, M., & Lane, H. R. (2004). *Education and peace.* Clio Press.

Montessori, M. (2017). *Maria Montessori Speaks to Parents: A Selection of Articles.* Amsterdam, The Netherlands: Montessori-Pierson Publishing Company.

Montessori, M., & Haines, A. M. (2018). *The 1946 London Lectures.* Montessori-Pierson Publishing Company.

Montessori, M., Juler, C., & Schulz-Benesch, G. (2016). In *The Child, Society and the World* (p. 44). essay, Montessori-Pierson Publishing Company.

Morin, A. (2020, September 22). *Establish Rules that Will Help Your Child Become a Responsible Adult.* Very well Family. Retrieved November 7, 2021, from https://www.verywellfamily.com/types-of-rules-kids-need-1094871

What is the Whole Child Approach? Professional Learning Board RSS. (n.d.). Retrieved December 13, 2021, from https://k12teacherstaffdevelopment.com/tlb/what-is-the-whole-child-approach/

Wolf, A. (2005). *Montessori Insights for Parents of Young Children.* Santa Rosa: Parent Child Press.

Suggested Resources

Harman, D. (2018). *Intentional Connections: A Practical Guide to Parent Engagement in Early Childhood & Lower Elementary Classrooms*. Parent Child Press.

Social and Podcast

www.facebook.com/DorothyHarmanEducatorandAuthor

www.intentionalconnections.buzzsprout.com/

For Ideas on Discipline in the Classroom and Home:

Nelsen, J., & Lorenzo, C. (2021). *Positive Discipline in the Montessori Classroom*. Parent Child Press.

Seldin, T., & McGrath, L. (2021). *Montessori for Every Family: A Practical Parenting Guide to Living, Loving, and Learning*. DK.

For More Inspiration:

Steindel, B. R. H. (2007). *The Call to Brilliance: A True Story to Inspire Parents and Educators*. Fredric Press.

Acknowledgments

My deepest appreciation to the amazing Montessorians, traditional educators, and parents who supported this book project, the Parent and Educator webinar series and Intentional Connections- the podcast.

Raegan Vanderplas & Jess Stanley

Donna May Tomboc & Jasmin Fiel-Samson

Jonathan Wolff & Stacey MacKinnon

Nancy Smith & Emily Kimm

Kim Boyd & Andrea Otte

Kitty Bravo & Katrina Kumar

Virginie Butin & Cassey Wesnofske

Cassi Mackey & Karen Lirange

Resa Steindel Brown & Erin Urwin

Anne Headley

Jackie Ostronic

Lynette Rohlfs

I also wish to express my most sincere gratitude to Joe Campbell whose friendship, guiding wisdom, writing acumen, vision, and faith in me have given me wings to fly! And to Carol Sapp for the butterflies that give that flight an image. And to Jane Campbell and my Parent Child Press and Montessori Services family, thank you for sharing so many gifts with the Montessori community and me.

About the Author

Dorothy Harman is an AMS EC credentialed Montessori guide and a retired public school Montessorian. She holds a BA in Early Childhood Education, a M. Ed. in Curriculum and Instruction and a M. Ed in Curriculum and Instruction with an Emphasis in Integrative Creative Arts. She serves as an Instructional Guide, Practicum Advisor and Field Consultant for the Center for Guided Montessori Studies and as Montessori consultant and Adjunct Lecturer at the University of Nebraska-Kearney. She is the Curriculum Coordinator at De La Fontaine Trilingual Montessori School and was a 2018 recipient of an AMS Peace Seed Grant. She is the author of *Intentional Connections: A Practical Guide to Parent Engagement in Early Childhood and Lower Elementary Classrooms* and *Intentional Connections: Building Parent Teacher Partnerships* published through Parent Child Press.

She lives with her husband Chris in sunny Florida where she enjoys visiting the beach with her children and extended family (Anthony and Chey, Alicia and Chris, Katina and Pascal, Lara, Adelya, and Nevia) and anyone else interested in gathering seashells and looking for dolphins.

When she is not guiding children, adult learners and families, Dorothy enjoys writing, public speaking, performing with her rock n' roll band, riding her purple motorcycle and dreaming about a jet ski!

www.ingramcontent.com/pod-product-compliance
Lightning Source LLC
Chambersburg PA
CBHW061344040426
42444CB00011B/3085